Great-Grandma Rose Krimsky

Her Story from 1915-2012

Contents

Biography of Grandma Rose Krimsky
1915 - 2012

*H*er life, struggles, and interactions with
her sons, grandchildren, great-grandchildren
and accomplishments of Grandma Rose.

Eulogy for Professor Sheldon Krimsky 1941 - 2022
Prepared by her son Sidney Krimsky, 2024
Prepared for the three children named after Grandma Rose
Shoshana Reizel Krimsky
Yakira Sara Rose Krimsky
Siona Rose Krimsky

Prologue:

This book is about the life of Rose (Skolnick) Krimsky known in her later years as Grandma Rose.

Orphaned in Ukraine, she was sponsored by her father to immigrate to America. He left Ukraine the day she was born. She arrived at Ellis Island in 1928 13 years old with almost no education in Russian Yiddish or Hebrew studies. The Bolsheviks saw to that. She and her husband Alex who arrived in 1924 with also little education could only watch while their children achieved the American Dream. The two boys graduated high school, college, married, bought homes, acquired professional employment, and had children that graduated college. Rose and Alex took pride in the accomplishments of their children and grandchildren. She doted on her children, grandchildren and her great grand-children as they grew up. Her name will be perpetuated into the next century and beyond.

Naming

From her Birth to Marriage, she is Rose.

From Marriage after birth of her first son, she is mom.

From birth of her first son after the birth of her first grandson, she is Grandma Rose.

Purpose

This biography is prepared for the three girls named after Grandma Rose who should know the life history after whom they were named. They are Yakira Sara Rose, daughter of Rabbi Elly and Yocheved Krimsky, Shoshana Reizel, daughter of Rabbi Jonathan and Cheryl (Chaya) Krimsky, and Siona Rose daughter of Eliot and Lisa Bengar Krimsky. The contents of this biography were personally told to me by Grandma Rose and from the contents of a letter written to Sheldon Krimsky by Uncle Munya December 1990 translated from the Russian language. I only regret that I did not to ask my aunts who emigrated from Ukraine about their lives, struggles, anxieties, and expectations about leaving Ukraine. I included a brief biography of Prof Sheldon Krimsky for Siona Rose Krimsky, his grand-daughter.

Early Childhood In Ukraine

We think **Raizel Shkolnikof** was born around 1915 in the village of Bieleh South of Yampol in Southern Ukraine. Her name was later anglicized to Rose. She did not possess a birth certificate. She arbitrarily selected 1 June as her birthday. Her mother was Chaya Sarah Shkolnikof and her father was Yitzhak Shkolnikof son of Meir. (Anglicized to Meyer). Meyer arrived in the USA in 1904 and lived in New York. Meyer had a pushcart, collected and sold rags. Isadore Skolnick was born on November 15 1988 in Ukraine. He became a naturalized citizen, record no. 43991. In the Hebrew language Raizel means Rose. The abbreviation (RZL) in Hebrew means "Our Rabbis of Blessed Memory" but this not a reason for her name.

A Torah Scroll and cover was dedicated to Raizel that resides in the ark (Aron in Hebrew) at the ECC Synagogue in West Hempstead. Yitzy and Naomi Hollander paid for the writing of the Torah and the beautiful mantel (cover) with Grandma Rose's and Grandma Reisman's Hebrew name. (Figure 1) The words on the mantle are from a verse in the Torah (Deuteronomy 32:19) that contains the commandment to write a Torah. It says "and now you write for yourselves that this poem (the Torah) for an Aliya (ascension) of the soul of Sheina Devorah the daughter of Rav Yitzhak Yaakov." (Yitzy's grandmother). The ע"ה stands for "woman of valor" and םולשה הילע which means let peace be upon her which basically is a synonym of may she rest in peace for ascension of the soul of Reizel the daughter of Yitzchak (Isadore) son of Meir. (Grandma Rose was Naomi's grandmother.) There is significance, reverence, honor, and respect for the deceased by providing a Torah in their name.

Rose's father Yitzhak Shkolnikof left Bieleh on the day she was born. Her mother Chaya Sarah Shkolnikof died, when Rose was about 4 years old perhaps from the Spanish Influenza that spread in Europe. Mom told me that her mother was covered in white and was placed on a wooden board on the floor with a burning candle above her head on the floor. Rose was now an orphan raised by the two sisters of her mother and one uncle; Aunt Raisa and Uncle Yossel Nischevitz. I will call her Rose until she becomes a mother and later grandmother. She had torn shoes and was not able to attend school on a regular basis. She had little education in reading or writing the Russian or Yiddish language but learned to speak those languages. She told me that during the cold winters a lamb was brought into the wooden house and a section of the house was roped off for the lamb that was shorn of wool at the end of winter and the wool was sold. She also remembered that her uncle waved a live chicken around his head before the holiday of Yom Kippur. This is done in accordance with the ancient Jewish tradition called "Kapparot meaning atonements" or sacrificing the chicken for the sins of the person before Yom Kippur. You pray for the sins to be forgiven.

Rose's father (Isadore) in America told me that he worked to send money to bring Rose to America but the broker stole the money. Yitzhak Shkolnikof, later anglicized his name to Isadore Skolnick, remarried Anna Matz on 6 March 1922 in Kings County Marriage Certificate 3001, who migrated from Poland to Canada and later to the USA. She and Isadore had three children, Ida (named after an aunt in Russia) who was born in 1920 and died in 2018 at age 98 from Covid infected by her aide. The next was Nathan born (guess) in 1922 and died about 20 years ago in Albuquerque, NM. He was

drafted and served as a driver in France during WWII. The third child was Harry (Heshy) and was born (guess) in 1927. He was drafted or joined the US Navy near the end of WWII. He died during the 1994 earthquake in Northridge, LA California. After WWII, he gave me a book about the Navy's activities during WWII.

Isadore sent money a second time to bring Rose to the USA. The broker hired a couple , who had two children, to accompany Rose on the train going to the ship that was to leave for America. Rose's two aunts were supposed to pack pillow cases and sheets to take to America because her aunts did not believe these were available in America. The bundles were never given to Rose. She traveled on the train and on the ship with only the clothes on her back. She had no money.

Leaving for America

The couple, their two children and Rose who travelled with them were all examined for communicable diseases especially for the contagious diseases such as lice, trachoma, etc. before boarding the ship. People with communicable diseases were denied access to board the ship. Adults were questioned about how much money they had, who is their sponsor, where they were going to live, how will they support themselves and do they plan to remain in America? Rose was not listed on the ship's manifest. She arrived as a WOP meaning "Without Papers." There is no documentation that she arrived in the USA. My brother Sheldon and I searched Ellis Island records and visited the National Archives in Washington DC several times. We spent hours looking at microfilm and found no evidence of her arrival on any ship's manifest. Rose lived in the steerage section on the ship and she wondered around. There was food available in the steerage section. No one took an interest in her. After two weeks on the ocean, the ship arrived at Ellis Island in 1928.

Her father took the ferry from Battery Park to Ellis Island and waited at the bottom of the stairs on the dock. Isadore knew when the ship would arrive. He sent a photo of himself to Rose in Ukraine. Rose became seasick and remained in the infirmary for a few days. She was not allowed to leave Ellis Island as a sick person. Isadore returned a few days later with a relative and they walked upstairs to the Great Hall to find his daughter. He saw a young girl and asked if she was Raizel Shkolnikof. She had no documentation. She knew her name and he told her that he was her father. They walked downstairs, took the ferry to Battery Park, and took the subway to his apartment in Williamsburg on Siegel Street. She was nervous leaving Ellis Island with a person she never met. She met her stepmother, Anna Matz. Later, they moved to 456 Alabama Avenue in East New York. Figure 2.

Arrival and Living in America

Her stepmother expected Rose to assist around the house including changing Heshy's diapers who was born 6 months before Rose arrived in America. She denied Rose food. Rose was enrolled in public school and was placed in the third grade at age 13 and was promoted as she learned to master English and arithmetic until she reached the seventh grade at age 16. During her teenage years her stepmother denied her food and made life uncomfortable. Rose hated her step mother. Years later she called her stepmother a "petzutzah" which is a female version of "putz." It means stupid, nasty, or lacking basic human traits. I heard that term used frequently. The word Pustoi in Russian (пустой) means empty or deserted. Her father gave Rose pocket change to buy lunch at school. Unknowingly, she bought candy for lunch during her school years. She had no idea that she was becoming malnourished. Anna could not read English or sign her name in English. She could cook. Her father took her out of school at age 16 because he wanted her to work and contribute to the family expenses. Her teachers wanted her to stay in school and at least graduate from junior high school.

Rose took the subway to the Garment District in Lower Manhattan to seek work. She was hired as a cutter to trim excess lace from women's underwear. She contributed 50% of her earnings to her father. She used her earnings to buy nice clothing and possibly attract a husband. She was miserable living at home with her stepmother who denied her food. Her misery is described in the book "My Life as a Motherless Child" written by Sheldon Krimsky.

After working hours, she joined a Russian immigrant group and met Sonya (Feldman) Krimsky who immigrated from Tulchin in Ukraine in 1926 with two daughters, Rachil and Annuita. She lived with her husband Shlomo, three daughters named Annuita, Rachil and Paulina, and her son Elyusha who migrated with Paulina to America in 1924. Sonya's husband arrived alone in 1910 and worked to send money to bring his family to America. (Shlomo's name was Anglicized to Samuel.) Rose received a letter written in Yiddish from Aunt Raisa and Uncle Yossel from Ukraine but could not read Yiddish or write in Yiddish. The sisters wanted to know how she was doing in America. Rose felt bad that she could not answer the letter. Later Isadore hired a tutor but I don't know what she learned from the tutor. Isadore and Rose did not answer the letter. He had enough stress from his wife and working as a house painter. Rose ended her schooling in 1931. She was 16. Her father never spoke to me about Ukraine.

Munya, the oldest son of Bubbe Sonya Krimsky, told me that the family was poor after their father left. The girls begged for food in the street. Sonya found work as a cook in an orphanage in Tulchin, so the children would not starve, before immigrating to America. So the six immigrants lived in a large apartment in New York. An older son, Manos (Munya) , born in 1904, refused to immigrate to the USA. He was drafted into the Red Army in 1926 at age 22 and retired as a Major before WWII ended. I have copies of the awards he received while serving in the Red Army. Samuel died in 1930. Annuita (Anglicized to Annette) married Isadore (Izzy) Weisleder in 1932. The large apartment had an empty room. Rose told Sonya about her miserable experience living with her stepmother. Sonya invited Rose to live with them so she moved from 456 Alabama

Avenue, into another apartment. The two girls, Bubbe Sonya, and Elyosha (Elyusha in Hebrew) lived in the apartment.

Rose worked, contributed to the household expenses, and met young boys at the Russian Immigrant Club. She enjoyed living with Sonya and learned how to cook, bake and make gefilte fish. She was fussy and did not like most of the boys she met. Sonya suggested she meet Elyosha, her son (Anglicized to Alex) and possibly marry. Alex worked for Smilen Bros. as a fruit handler. They dated and decided to marry. Alex and Rose visited Isadore, her father who brought her from Ukraine to his home at 456 Alabama Avenue. Figure 3. Isadore had some Jewish education. Alex had none. The Bolsheviks demolished all the Jewish Schools. Isadore expected Rose to marry an educated Jewish boy. Isadore asked Alex about his Yichus "(Jewish genealogy)." Alex came to the US as a "muzhik" or uneducated peasant farmer or worker. Alex said to Isadore "Yichus-Tuches" which means "genealogy my ass." Isadore asked Alex and Rose to leave the apartment.

Getting Married and Living in East New York

They left and returned to announce they were getting married and asked Isadore to arrange the wedding and festive meal afterwards. They were married in the Shul across the street from Isadore's small apartment on 456 Alabama Avenue. The couple received about $60 in cash and some gifts. Isadore asked for half of the money to pay the caterer and cook. They were married on 20 January 1935. Alex and Rose spent one night at the Half Moon Hotel on West 29th Street in Coney Island. The Shul and Half-Moon Hotel no longer exist. The Shul was replaced by an apartment building across the street where our grandparents lived. Figure 4.

The newly married couple lived in a tenement on 217 Watkins Street in East New York until October 1936. Sidney was born on 17 March 1936. The bathroom was in the hallway shared by three families. Rodents roamed in the building. Alex worked and Mom managed the finances, shopped, cooked, and cleaned. Cleaning was done in a bathtub rubbing the clothes using a washboard and hanging up the washed clothes on a clothesline using wooden clothespins. She saved the washboard for me so I would know how hard she worked to keep us clean. I still have the washboard. They bought clothes on Pitkin Avenue.

We moved to 496 Williams Ave until Oct 1939. Figure 5. Then we moved to 637 Blake Ave to Sept 1940. Sheldon was born in June 1941. Then we moved to 169 Dumont Ave until Feb 1942. All the apartments were nearby. The Watkins Street, Blake Avenue, and Dumont Street buildings were demolished and replaced by large apartment buildings. The Alabama and Williams Avenue buildings still exist and have been rehabilitated. The clothing stores and kosher butcher shops on Pitkin Avenue no longer exist.

After the U.S. declared war on Japan in December 1941, the Baltimore Naval Shipyard was opened. Alex went to Baltimore to apply for work as a metal worker for the Baltimore Naval Shipyard. He was hired and then we moved to 255 Herring Court in Baltimore until November 1945. The shipyard was demobilized after the war ended. Then we moved to 2995 West 29th Street in Coney Island until 1970. I graduated from CCNY and left Coney Island in 1958 to work for Aerojet Corp. in Sacramento, California. The building was taken by the City by eminent domain and demolished by directives of Robert Moses, the czar of redlining neighborhoods, around 1972. In 1959 they moved to 2375 East 3rd Street near Avenue X in Brooklyn. After about two years they moved to Warbasse Housing sponsored by the ILGW near Ocean Parkway and Neptune Avenue. They were given a 3 room apartment on the 17th floor, Apt 17H. ILGWU means International Ladies Garment Workers Union.

Sidney Herman was born on 17 March 1936 and named after Rose's mother Chaya Sarah. Rose was malnourished during her teen-age years so Sidney was born with rickets, irregular pulse, thin arms and wrists and a sinus condition. A doctor recommended and Mom insisted that I take a tablespoon of Cod Liver oil every day to offset the rickets and play in the sun. Every day she would say "Sidney, open your mouth" and I would swallow a tablespoon of cod liver oil. I stopped at age 10. My legs were strong and appeared normal. Mom provided me with a daily handkerchief because I had a running nose in school. Sheldon was born 5 years later in June 1941 and did not have these medical issues. I had a circumcision but no "pidyan haben" (redemption of the first born) 30 days later in accordance with Jewish Law. Alex was circumcised in Bratislava, Ukraine in 1908. When Sidney was 3 or 4 years old Alex purchased a barabanchik (Russian) or "drummer-boy doll." Mom yelled at him for spending money on a toy when money was tight. I remember how she yelled at him. Alex also purchased a board with small holes, pegs, and a wooden small hammer. I learned to place the pegs in the holes and hit them with the hammer.

Moving to Baltimore, Maryland

On December 7, 1941 Japan bombed Pearl Harbor. The Baltimore Naval Shipyard was established in 1941 and closed in 1945. The Navy placed ads for shipyard workers in newspapers. Alex responded, by going to Baltimore and applying for work as a sheet metal worker. He was hired and then we moved to Baltimore in 1942 into new housing for shipyard workers. We moved from New York to 255 Herring Court which was about a mile to the shipyard. He did not need a car. Alex was employed as a metal worker. He even made his own wedding ring and a bracelet for Rose out of Monel (molybdenum alloy) which did not rust. We lived on the second floor of a two family house. The apartment was clean with a bathroom in the apartment. Mom loved the apartment. Annette's husband Izzy also found work in Baltimore and moved his family consisting of Stanley (named after Samuel Krimsky) and his daughter Elaine.

Mom went shopping for food on Lombard Street. There were ample grocery stores and kosher butchers. Mom bought wholesome vegetables, meat and fish. We ate no processed foods. She baked sponge cake, honey cake, apple pies and made delicious gefilta fish. The wooden bowl and chopper she used to chop the fish is shown in Figure 29. Also shown is the stool she used to access supplies on the upper cabinet shelves. She was barely 5 feet tall. The chopper, wooden bowl and stool are about 85 years old. She purchased no processed food. She recovered from her malnutrition during her teen-age years. She wheeled the baby carriage for Sheldon and put groceries in the carriage. Mom managed the finances and even saved $160 which was a lot of money at that time. Alex walked to work to the Baltimore Shipyard. He did not need a car. Mom was meticulous in checking the addition of all the prices for the food items. The prices were listed on the grocery bag. Years later she trusted me to do the math addition. Mom taught me to tie shoelaces by making a knotted bow with the shoelaces.

Sonya Krimsky paid a visit to help Mom with baby Sheldon. Ida Skolnick, before she married Perry Fishbein, visited us and we all took a train in June to Washington, DC. (Union Station) on a Sunday. We walked and saw the gargoyles on the fountain opposite the Senate Russell Building and walked into the open Rotunda of the US Capital. There were no police or guards and few people. Congress was not in session during the summer. We saw black people mopping the floors. We saw the statues in the Rotunda. Doors to the Congress, Senate, and offices were closed. We returned to Baltimore.

One day after work a stranger knocked on the door. Alex walked down the stairs and opened the door. A stranger but a co-worker at the shipyard said he missed his ride home and asked if he could have something to eat. I watched him from the second floor standing near the staircase. Alex understood and asked Mom to make a sandwich. Alex gave the man a sandwich and a glass of milk. He ate, thanked us, and left. We never saw him again.

One day Sidney woke up with a stiff neck and his neck was locked. Rose located a chiropractor near the shipyard and we walked to his office. The chiropractor sat behind a large desk and his back faced a large circular window with a view of Baltimore Harbor. He asked Mom a few questions, placed his large hands on both sides of my face and gave my head a quick twist. I felt no pain. He unlocked my neck and I could move my head in any direction. Mom paid his fee and we walked home. That never happened again. At age 6 years Mom enrolled me into public school and a Talmud Torah that I attended after school hours.

At the end of August 1945 we received a telegram that Bubbe Sonya Krimsky died. She had 6 grandchildren. The oldest, grandchild was named Salim (meaning Shalom in Russian). The only son of Munya and Frida, was born in 1930 in Baku and named after his grandfather Shalom (later anglicized to Samuel) who died earlier in 1930. Baku is the capital and largest city of Azerbaijan, as well as the largest city on the Caspian Sea and of the Caucasus region. Bubbe Sonya never met Salim. The other five grandchildren lived in New York and are Stanley, Elaine, Jerry, Sidney and Sheldon. Salim died in 2022 (at age 92) in Russia. Jerry died in 2010 (at 75 waiting for a kidney) in California and Sheldon died in 2022 (almost 81) in Cambridge, Massachusetts. Salim graduated college in Russia as a metallurgist however his first love was music. He studied music at night, wrote symphonies, and became a member of the prestigious Russian Composers Union. Stanley studied math and became an actuary and owned his own insurance company specializing in retirement accounts, Jerry became an accountant, and Sidney became an engineer and published 4 books after retirement in 2010. Sheldon became a college professor and published 14 books about science. Elaine majored in biochemistry and attended law school after college and became a judge in California. The third generation achieved the American Dream.

We took a train to New York and went to Isadore Skolnick's apartment on Alabama Avenue. Our parents left us with a baby sitter while they went to the funeral of Bubbe Sonya. We took the train back to Baltimore. We were fond of Bubbe Sonya. The war ended and the Baltimore Shipyard was de-activated in 1945. Alex's job would soon disappear. We had to move. Alex wanted to reconnect with his siblings.

Moving to Coney Island

A friend from New York or a distant relative located a 3 room empty apartment on West 29th Street in Coney Island. During WW II houses and apartments were not built. The economy including transportation was all part of winning the war. Bread and meat were in short supply since food products were sent overseas to support US soldiers. The Federal Government issued food stamps that were presented to grocers and butchers to avoid hoarding and black market profiteering. Stamps were freely issued by the post office that we had to present to the grocer and butcher. This effort was administrated by the OPA (Office of Price Administration) passed under Pres. Roosevelt to avoid profiteering. In 1945 or 1946 the hated OPA was abolished by Pres. Truman. Rose saved $160 living in Baltimore which was a lot of money at that time. She was able to purchase two beds, dressers, chairs, and a sofa bed for the new apartment in Coney Island.. She had an eye for buying good furniture at a reasonable price. Mom managed the family finances. Dad trusted her.

Once when we lived in Coney Island my father drove me to the gravesite of Bubbe Sonya his mother and his father Samuel. He arranged flowers on the bed of the gravesite. I was about 10 or 11 years old. They are buried in Mt Hebron Cemetery, near Main Street, in Queens.

So we moved to 2995 West 29th Street (Figure 30) in Coney Island into a small 3 room apartment that had a kitchen, living room in which Mom and Dad purchased a sofa that pulled out as a bed, one bedroom, and a bathroom. The bedroom had room for two beds, one for me, one for Sheldon, and a dresser. Our parents sacrificed by having us sleep in the one bedroom in two beds while they used a pull-away sofa in the living room. One window had a fire escape that looked out on the empty lot in back of the house and the other window looked out on the bungalow colony below. One window frame in the living room was somehow attached to a clothes line, the other post was a telephone pole. Mom taught me to wash my teeth by sprinkling a powder (I think baking soda) on the tooth brush. For the first time we bought and used Ipana brand toothpaste that we squeezed from a plastic tube. There was no spillage. Toothpaste was a wonderful invention.

School and Talmud Torah Enrollment

Mom walked with me to 35th Street and Neptune Avenue in Coney Island to enroll me in PS 188 (Public School). I was tested to determine my academic level. The tester advised Mom that I should enter the 5th grade and skip the 4th grade. I graduated from P.S. 188 at age 11 and entered Mark Twain Junior High School in an SP class that was college bound. I graduated from Mark Twain at age 14 and Abraham Lincoln High School at age 17 and 3 months. Mom went to visit Mark Twain Jr. High School during Open School Week and sat in the classroom and listened to Ms. Kehoe instruct the class. Mom attended all my graduations. Mom also enrolled me at the Sea Gate Sisterhood and Talmud Torah where I learned Hebrew, Yiddish, and the Haftorah for my bar mitzvah that was held in the Synagogue on West 23rd Street and Mermaid Avenue in Coney Island. I sat in the outer office when Mom negotiated tuition for attending the Talmud Torah with Rabbi Judah Galinsky. The tuition was settled at a few dollars per week because we were poor.

Between 1947 to 1948, the teachers at the Sea Gate Sisterhood and Talmud Torah asked the students to collect food from the residents of Coney Island to be sent to Israel. We were told that people were emigrating from Europe to Israel and needed food. We were not told the extent of the Holocaust. The teachers assigned two boys to sections of Coney Island. I and another student were assigned to the large apartment building on 28th Street and Surf Avenue in which many Jewish families lived. We had a red wagon and knocked on doors telling people who we were and that we were collecting food for Israel. Many people were home, answered the door bell, and gave us canned food. I told mom what we were doing and she donated two cans of food. She was really proud that we were doing this. I recall that Del Monte fruit and vegetables were popular donations. We trundled the wagon filled with cans of food on Surf Avenue to Mermaid Avenue to West 23rd Street to the Talmud Torah. Adults packed the cans into boxes, put the boxes on to pallets, and placed the pallets onto a waiting truck. The truck brought the pallets to a dock on the Hudson River and then lifted them on a ship sailing to Israel. The trip lasted about two weeks and much later I learned that the food was unloaded at the port of Haifa. The boys in my Hebrew Class collected food for the Holocaust survivors who came to Israel after WW II ended.

Railroad Avenue

Between Mermaid and Surf Avenues there was a parallel street called Railroad Avenue. Trolley tracks started from the subway station at Stillwell Avenue, over Gargulio's Restaurant, and ended at Tompkins Square in Sea Gate. The ride costs 5 or 10 Cents. During the cold and dark winter months Mom insisted that I take the trolley from 23rd street (location of the Talmud Torah) to 29th street. She gave me the fare. Sometimes I walked and saved the fare money. . In the summer my friends and I placed pennies on the trolley tracks and watched the heavy wheels crush the pennies into flat metal. It was amusing for us. I wish I had saved the flattened pennies. Nickels were too valuable to be treated in this manner. A few years later the trolleys stopped running and were replaced by busses that started from underneath the subway station at Stillwell Avenue and traveled along Surf Avenue to Sea Gate but not inside Sea Gate.

At PS 188, in the 5th and 6th grades I was given homework assignments to write about various subjects. Since my parents had little education, they could not help me. We had no books in the house. My father would drive me to the Coney Island Public Library on Mermaid Avenue and West 16th Street after he returned from work. Some of my classmates boasted about having the Encyclopedia Britannica at home. It was the most advanced reference book at the time. I felt a little jealous. One day a large box arrived at home that contained all the books of the New Standard Encyclopedia. Wow! I perused through the books looking mostly at the pictures and my world opened up. I could write reports about any subject. Mom and Dad paid hard earned money to buy the encyclopedia. I never asked for it knowing their financial situation but they realized the importance of a good education. Mom was never allowed to finish junior high school. Dad was not interested in personal education. He bought a book called "Audel's Machinist and Tool Makers Handbook" and tried at night in Baltimore to read the book to improve his employment as a metal worker but it was too difficult. He had no education and the algebra was impossible for him to understand. I still have the book. He realized that education was key to advancement. He learned to read and write by copying words from the New York newspapers.

Watching Television

We could not afford a TV. Mom asked a neighbor, Clarisse, if Sheldon and I could watch TV in her immaculate apartment. She agreed so every Tuesday night we showered, ate supper, and walked upstairs at 8:00 PM to watch Milton Berle and at 9:00 PM to watch the Texaco Star Theater which was a mystery program. I remember watching a mystery program called "The Monkey's Paw" which was scary. Milton Berle was a very popular comedian and was responsible for the sale of millions of TV sets. Movies lost customers on Tuesday nights and gave away dishes to attract customers.

About 1952 our Aunt Rae purchased a TV set for us because Mom testified that Rae's husband Meyer was unfaithful and Rae (Alex's sister) wanted a divorce. Alex and his sisters urged her to testify falsely because Rae wanted a divorce. Rae hoped that Vincent, a truck driver, would ask her for marriage. He did not ask. Rae could not have children. Her insides were messed up. Later we learned that Meyer moved to Canada, remarried and had children. We never saw him again. I liked Uncle Meyer. Years later Mom told me that she always regretted giving false testimony in court about Uncle Meyer. She did not want to upset our relationship with Alex's sisters. She talked about it all the time because it bothered her but Alex and his sisters urged her to do this. Divorces were not easily granted at that time. It really bothered her.

During the years at P.S. 188 I was given spelling assignments for homework. I asked mom to read the words on my assignment list and I would recite the letters. Later in Jr. High School I asked her to test me on words I had to translate into French. She read the English words and I recited the translation into French.

We did not have excess financial resources but Mom always bought unprocessed food for meals. She taught me to only take what I could finish. I could take as much food as I wanted but shouldn't leave any food over. That would be wasteful. The left-over food would have to be discarded. That stayed with me.

Singing in a Jewish Choir

During the late summer of 1947 the boys on the block where we lived were approached by Elchik Conviser, who lived across the street from where we lived. He asked us if anyone wanted to join a choir to sing at various Shuls (synagogues) for the three high holidays. We would be paid for our participation. I was interested and was told I had to go to his apartment to be tested for voice, pitch and if I could I follow a melody. My voice had not yet changed. Four boys named Bobby Schwartz, Ronald Rosenberg, Steven Stein and I were hired. We were hired to sing songs based on the holiday services. The melodies for the songs were written by Mr. Conviser. We had rehearsals every Thursday night in August. I sang duets with Bobby Schwartz and Steven Stein sang solo. He had a beautiful tenor voice. We were driven to the various Shuls (in Brownsville and East New York). Mom knew all about this and insisted that she buy new appropriate dress clothes for me. I did not think I needed a new suit but she insisted. She did not want me looking like a shlump (slob) singing in a synagogue during the high holidays. So we went to Mirsky's clothing store on Pitkin Avenue and bought new clothes. I told her that we were peasants and wearing new clothes could not change that. I was paid $35 for the three High Holidays which was a lot of money in 1947. Food was provided by the families who volunteered to host us. The Conviser choir was deactivated around 1950 so Sheldon never had a chance to sing the Hebrew songs in a choir.

Although we lived one block from the ocean, mom never entered the ocean. She rarely went to the beach. She was not interested in learning how to drive a Car. It was rare for women to drive cars in those days. We were surprised to learn that her step-sister Ida, learned to drive on a Hydra-Matic car. They became more available after WWII. I learned to drive in a car with a clutch. None of my father's siblings learned to drive.

I learned to swim after one lesson by my father. Mom was afraid of the ocean because she was thrown into a lake in Russia. She underestimated me and my mental and physical abilities. Don't jump off the boardwalk onto the sand. Don't jump between the roofs in the bungalow colonies on Surf Avenue. I did all that. At age 11 or 12 I wanted to take my younger brother to Ebbets Field to watch the Brooklyn Dodgers play the Pittsburgh Pirates. She worried I would get lost using the subway. I knew my way around the subway. We went to Ebbets Field and did not get lost. The subways cost around 15 cents and were safe.

Several times a year we were invited to the home of Annette & Izzy Weisleder for a Sunday Breakfast served with bagels, lox, cream cheese, etc. They lived in a beautiful home in the Sheepshead Bay area in Brooklyn. Izzy worked as a grocer, had a great sense of humor and always told funny stories. Our three other cousins, Elaine, Stanley & Jerry, their parents and Aunt Rae were there. We never heard about Uncle Munya and Cousin Salim who lived in Russia. I sensed that Mom felt a little jealous that although we enjoyed these breakfasts, she felt inadequate to reciprocate. Our relatives from Europe tried to keep the family together. Elaine passed away in June 2024.

Walking to Zadie's Shul

My brother agreed to accompany me on Yom Kippur to walk with me to our grandfather's Synagogue (Shul) on Pennsylvania Avenue in East New York near Blake Avenue. I was 13 and he was 8 years old. Attending Synagogue Services in the Shul on Yom Kippur located on Surf Avenue and West 28th Street was of little interest to me although I did fast for the day in accordance with Jewish Law. I asked Mom to allow Sheldon to come with me. She agreed. After Sheldon ate lunch, we walked on Surf Avenue to Ocean Parkway, to Kings Highway, to Linden Boulevard, then North on Pennsylvania Avenue toward Blake Avenue. The distance was about 9.4 miles. It took almost 4 hours. We walked into the Shul during Neilah (end of the service) and our grandfather could not believe that we walked that distance. He was amazed and said he will never forget this day. After the service ended we walked to his apartment on Alabama Avenue and called home. CO 6 -1950 (CO was Coney Island) which was our phone number. Our father drove us home after we ate a light supper. I knew all the streets because I studied a street map of New York. Mom always underestimated me. I was the oldest grandchild and Zadie doted on me. Once he invited me to stay a few days at his bungalow in the Catskill Mountains. He arranged for a friend to be with me and I learned how to fish. Bubbe Skolnick did all the cooking.

My Bar-Mitzvah

At age 13, Mom insisted that we should have a big bar-mitzvah party and she arranged for a celebration at the Melrose Chateau, I think, off Coney Island Avenue in Brooklyn. Mom was so impressed with my speech in Yiddish that I delivered at the Shul for my bar-mitzvah that she wanted me to make a record of my speech. So we went to Grand Central Station to a recording studio and made a 45 rpm record. We met Uncle Meyer, husband of Aunt Rae. He worked at a candy store concession somewhere in Grand Central Station that also sold newspapers and magazines. He was married to Rae at the time. The Synagogue, Hebrew School, (Sea Gate Sisterhood and Talmud Torah) and Melrose Chateau Hall no longer exist. Figure 6. She told Sheldon (in his book) that she did not arrange a big bar mitzvah party for Sheldon for two reasons. One reason was cost because money was tight. The second reason was that Mom did not want her stepmother to attend any family simchas (celebrations). There was a small synagogue service in a small Shul on 35th Street (I think) in Coney Island. Isadore Skolnick came and walked to our apartment from the Shul. But he was not happy that his wife was not invited. Mom prepared a dinner for our relatives on our father's side to observe Sheldon's bar mitzvah. The living room became a dining room. There was no larger celebration for his bar mitzvah as was mine at the Melrose

Chateau. I never thought about the inequality of treatment until I grew older. After his bar-mitzvah, Sheldon had no further interest in the Jewish traditions. He never travelled to Israel.

Coney Island Living

Mom used the bathtub and a washboard to wash clothes until washing machines were brought to the basement of the house on 29th Street. Mom hung up washed clothes to dry on the clothesline. The basement had storage space with locked bins for the tenants use. Mom bought chunks of beef and put them into a meat grinder that had a large Archimedean screw and a large handle. The beef emerged in long strings that she cut, mashed, and broiled to make hamburgers and meat loaf. I always volunteered to disassemble the meat grinder and clean the moving parts. I liked to take things apart. I still have the meat grinder and washboard we can use in case we lose electricity. Figure 28.

Alex learned how to paint and worked as a house painter. He stored his tools, paint, and brushes in the basement in a locked storage bin for the tenant's use. On occasion I used his tools to make things out of wood. I watched him work around the house and rewire lamps. I learned how to do that. I made WW II airplanes from balsa wood and hung them above my bed. The model airplanes cost $0.25. I earned money by returning used Coke bottles I found on the beach receiving 5 cents for each bottle returned. There were kiosks under the boardwalk that sold and received used bottles. Sheldon and I received Chanukah Money from Isadore Skolnick, our grandfather who visited us every year during Chanukah time. Mom encouraged me to open a bank account and I did with their signatures in the Coney Island Savings Bank. The kiosks no longer exist. The space under the boardwalk was filled with sand. I heard that the space and kiosks under the boardwalk were used for drugs.

During the hot summer months we went swimming in the ocean but not far from the beach. At many sites along the beach, there were three barrels each anchored to the ocean bottom about 50 feet apart. There were ropes between the barrels to enable a swimmer to pull him or herself back to the beach. We used to swim out to the third barrel, dive down into the water, look for sea shells, and swim back to the beach or pull ourselves forward by holding the ropes. The barrels are no longer there.

Once I returned home from the beach and my back was covered with blisters. It was a really hot day. My back burned and Mom called Dr. Kravitz who had an office on 29th Street and Mermaid Avenue. He drove his car and parked outside our house. He came up the stairs. He was dressed with a suit and tie, holding a black bag. He used his stethoscope and examined me. I had severe sunburn. He recommended a special cream, told me not to go to the beach for a few days, and told me to wear a white T-shirt when I am on the beach because the sunburn could return. Mom paid him two dollars for a house call. An office call cost one dollar. Mom went to Benny Siegel's Pharmacy on the corner of 29th Street and Surf Avenue, bought the special cream and applied it gently to my back. The blisters disappeared in a few days.

Sam and Clara Dauer lived across the courtyard in our building. Clara asked Mom if I would be able to write letters that she dictated to her son who lived in Fargo, North Dakota. Clara was a refugee unschooled in writing English. Mom agreed but I would have to be clean before entering their apartment. I agreed and was paid 50 cents per letter that started with "Dear Harry and Bert" and ended with an appropriate goodbye. I did this once a week until I completed High School and then Sheldon replaced me. Sam Dauer was wheelchair bound and lived above the first floor in the building with no elevator. He sat and watched TV most of the time. I never saw him outside. The word "Dauer" in German means to last and they lasted until the 1970s when the building was taken by eminent domain and eventually demolished. The building space is now used as a community garden for nearby residents.

Cigarettes and Smoking

Mom never asked us to buy cigarettes for Alex, our father. She insisted that he smoke outside of our apartment. The air was smoke-free in our apartment but Alex's clothes reeked of cigarette smoke. He started to smoke in Russia as a young boy to lessen stomach pain from lack of food. He smoked Camel Cigarettes. The advertising signs in the New York Subways said that "More Doctors Smoked Camel Cigarettes than any other Cigarette." Figure 7. At that time, smoking was allowed on the subways. I always believed that putting anything in your lungs and paying for it was irrational and stupid so I never even tried it. The MTA (Metropolitan Transit Authority) in New York finally banned all cigarette smoking in subways in 1988. Smoking was also banned on airplanes. Later I learned that all the medical reports saying that cigarette smoke was not harmful were all lies.

My brother Sheldon was once bullied at Mark Twain Jr. High School. Mom asked me to do something. I found the name and address of the bully and visited his parents. I provided them with the phone number of Coney Island Hospital where he would be found if he continued to bully my younger brother. I was 16 or 17 at the time. The bullying stopped.

After graduating CCNY in 1958 I accepted employment in Sacramento, California as a development engineer for the Aerojet Corporation. My biography is described in my first published book "From Brooklyn, NY to Brookline, MA". I learned to ski in California. In 1959 I observed the downhill ski racing at Squaw Valley during the winter Olympics. In 1960 I left Aerojet and moved to Cambridge, Massachusetts to work in many high tech firms. In 1961 Paul Mermelstein and I went on a ski trip to Mt. Snow in Vermont. The road was slippery with snow and I had a head-on collision with another car. My jaw hit the steering wheel, was fractured, and several teeth were broken. We were transported by ambulance to Mass General Hospital. The trip cost $100 and I paid the driver with cash. I think that Paul broke his nose. I spent two nights in the hospital and Dr. Peter Kimball wired my jaw. Mom came to my apartment and prepared liquid food so I had something to eat because my jaw was wired shut to allow the wound to heal. She stayed for about 3-4 days until the doctor unwired my jaw. I went back to work with a wired jaw and drank my lunch from a thermos bottle.

Figure 8 shows Grandma Rose, Alex, Sheldon, and Sidney standing on the John Weeks Bridge overlooking the Charles River in Cambridge, MA that connects Cambridge with Allston, a suburb of Boston in May 1965. Mom and Dad came to attend to my graduation ceremony from Northeastern University where I earned an MSME degree.

Meeting and Marrying Dorothy Goldstein

In June 1965 I met Dorothy Goldstein at a party for graduate students attending MIT. The place for the party was called "Middlesex House" because Cambridge was in Middlesex County. Dorothy's brother Albert was a physics major at MIT and we went on hiking trips together. Marvin Koren, a part-time MIT graduate student, introduced me to the group. He and I worked at the Geophysics Corporation of America on different projects. A week or two later I saw Dorothy Saturday afternoon standing in front of the Harvard Coop and suggested we go out. She said that she had a play date with two girls and would have to ask them. I suggested we all go out to the Cape Cod Canal for a picnic lunch and I would drive my car. She called me later and said her friends agreed so I drove the three girls to Cape Cod. They sat in the back and talked and giggled during the trip. I drove Dorothy home later and she agreed to go out a second time. In March 1966 I called my mother and told her that I was engaged. She asked me if I was drunk. Marvin, his future wife Isabel, Dorothy and I climbed Mt Washington n the Fall of 1965. Unfortunately, Marvin Koren passed away June 2024.

On Saturday evening I drove Dorothy to meet Mom and Dad and I met Dorothy's parents, Frank and Belle Goldstein. My relatives came over on Sunday to meet Dorothy. Mom was pleased and took an immediate liking to Dorothy. Her parents arranged the marriage for 14 August 1966 at the Regency House in Queens. The building was later demolished. All my aunts, uncles, and cousins from my father's side were invited. None of the relatives from my mother's side were invited because of their dislike of Mom because of her hatred for her step-mother, the "petzutzah." Mom never forgot and never forgave her. I decided to invite Isadore Skolnick, my grandfather whom we called Zadie, and his wife. Mom objected to inviting the "petzutzah." She said she would not attend the wedding if the petzutzah were invited. I suggested she stay home because not inviting my Zadie's wife is a great insult. I wanted no part of that. Bubbe Skolnick treated me with respect over the years although we did not communicate. The "petzutzah" came and sat at a distant table. My Zadie made the brocha (blessing) over the Challeh (special bread). There were no further discussions about this matter.

We honeymooned in Canada and visited Niagara Falls, Montreal, and Quebec. We returned to an apartment on Summit Avenue in Brighton and joined an orthodox synagogue, Kadimah –Toras Moshe. Dorothy set up our apartment and she completed her education by enrolling at Northeastern University for an MA in Secondary School Counseling. She graduated in June 1967. Mom and I attended her graduation ceremony.

Death of Alex Krimsky

lex stopped painting houses because the effort to paint, especially ceilings with a brush, was too strenuous so he applied and received a New York City taxi license. During the evenings he would drive to Tony and Mike's gas station and garage on Neptune Avenue near Stillwell in Coney Island just to socialize and sometimes give gas to customers. Mom was busy shopping, cooking and cleaning. Sheldon and I were preoccupied in school. Watching TV was limited because I did my homework in the living room where the TV was located. One day Alex blacked out while driving and surrendered his taxi license. He still drove his own car. He sat on the benches outside the new residence on 235 Neptune Avenue after moving from 2995 West 29th Street. On the day of lighting the 6th candle of Chanukah, my Aunt Annette called and told me that Alex died. I could not believe it. I drove that night with Dorothy and Sheldon to our parents' home to attend to the funeral the next day. I saw him in lying in repose in the funeral parlor. I expected him to get up and walk around as he always did. He was buried in Mountefiore Cemetery off Springfield Boulevard in the neighborhood of St. Albans, Queens. He was the first of the five Russian siblings to die. Mom was a widow for 46 years and lived alone. Alex never saw his grandchildren. He was born in 1908 and was 58 years old when he died. He married at age 27. Mom was 52 years old when he died. We think she was born in 1915 and 20 years old when she married Alex in 1935. Eulogies are in the book "From Brooklyn, NY to Brookline, MA." Grandpa Alex never saw his grandchildren.

After Alex died, Dorothy became pregnant and our first son was born 30 May 1968. I called my mom, and told her that she would be known as Grandma Rose from that time. We named him Alec Seth after my father. I could not bear calling him Alex. In the Torah, Adam had another son and named him Seth, another child, in place of Abel for Cain slew him. I viewed Alec as a kind of substitute for Alex to sooth my soul. Mom was thrilled, attended his bris milah and 30 days later his pidyon haben (redemption of the first born). I gave Max Katz, the cousin of Alex Krimsky, who was a Kohain five silver dollars to redeem Alec that I purchased at the Harrah's Club near Lake Tahoe in Nevada just across the State Line from California. Some force compelled me to buy five silver dollars in the winter of 1959 nine years before Alec was born.

Move to Newton, Massachusetts in 1995

Grandma Rose was feisty and did not want to depend on children. Alex died too young to receive any social security benefits. She found work in the garment district in lower Manhattan repairing women's dresses. She prepared breakfast, a bag lunch, walked to the Neptune Avenue and West 6th Street Subway Station, climbed up the long staircase five times each week and prepared supper. She shopped for food on weekends or holidays. She asked Sheldon to be her health care proxy and financial advisor. Work became too much for her at age 61 or 62 and Sheldon assisted her to apply for social security benefits. Grandma Rose was mugged twice and it was time to move. Sheldon suggested that she move closer to Boston where we both lived and Sheldon's daughter Alyssa lived in nearby Arlington. However Mom had many friends where she loved and attended Sabbath Services at the Ocean Parkway Synagogue , only a few blocks away from her apartment on Neptune Avenue. Sheldon applied for housing for Grandma Rose at the newly built Golda Meir Housing for the elderly in Newton, Massachusetts. He submitted an application for a lottery. Many people applied. Rabbi Abraham Halbfinger, who was the Rabbi of our Congregation, contacted the management people at the Golda Meir Housing and wrote a letter strongly recommending that she be accepted. She waited about 2 ½ years before acceptance. Her friends and neighbors made a going away party at Ratner's Restaurant on the lower

East Side of Manhattan that we attended. Grandma Rose had many neighborly friends in New York and friends from the different local organizations in which she volunteered. She was a secretary taking notes of meetings, interacting with the members, and recording attendance. This gave her purpose after the death of her husband and departure of her two children to Massachusetts. Moving her to Massachusetts means she lost her friends and had to make new friends. Dorothy and I were employed and busy. Carolyn lived in New York. Sheldon spent time in New York and Cambridge as an employed professor and author. We could not visit her on a weekly basis. Figure 9.

Death of Isadore Skolnick (Our Zadie)

We visited Zaydie after he moved from Alabama Avenue to Fountain Avenue helped by his daughter Ida Fishbein. Aunt Ida told me that he was the Mayor of Alabama Avenue. He knew all the Jewish residents on the street and their problems. The Jewish residents slowly disappeared from Alabama Avenue to be replaced by Hispanics. Alec was about 2 years old. We paid a visit to Fountain Avenue. Zaydie said that he would not be able to attend his bar mitzvah. He knew that he would not be alive in 11 years. He was born in 1888. Naomi was born in 1970 around Purim. I called Zadie to tell him that Naomi had red hair. He said that his cousin "Nachum der Roita" or Nathan the Red-Haired One died and was now "Nachum der Toita" (in Yiddish) or Nathan the dead one. It was a great liner and a laughable moment. Zadie died suddenly after Passover. I went to his funeral, met his three children, and went to the cemetery. None of his grandchildren attended. He told me that he painted the gate to his gravesite with red paint so people could find it. I spray painted the gate red every time I visited the Montefiore Cemetery. All his children are deceased. No one visits his gravesite any longer. He was 82. His wife was moved to the Haber House for seniors located in Coney Island near the boardwalk and I visited her once. She was not very verbal and we had nothing to say. She told me that she missed her husband. She died a few years later. Grandma Rose told me a week after the funeral, to ensure that I did not attend, so I did not attend the funeral. I would have gone had I known the date and place of the funeral.

Marriage of Sheldon Krimsky and Carolyn Boriss

Grandma Rose told me that Sheldon was looking for a girl who was not concerned with money. Sheldon was an academic person disinterested in earning a living just to earn lots of money. He met Carolyn Boriss, an art major at Brooklyn College. She had no interest in Jewish traditions. We employed a baby sitter to look after Alec and Naomi during the wedding. At the wedding, Sheldon gave me a goblet filled with champagne and asked me to make a toast to the married couple to wish them happiness and success in their endeavors. I had the words in my head when Sheldon approached me and said that Carolyn wanted Patrick to make the toast so I gave him the goblet and Patrick made a toast. Patrick was married to Carolyn's sister and they divorced after a few years. So much for Patrick! Eve Boriss was Carolyn's mother and Mac Boriss was her deceased father who was a business man. I did not realize it then but this was the beginning of a fractured relationship. Grandma Rose told me that Carolyn did not get along with her father. Grandma Rose told me that when Carolyn's mother died, Carolyn inherited the funds from the sale of the house and maintained a private bank account.

Eve Boriss. Carolyn's mother, invited Sheldon, Carolyn, and Grandma Rose to a dinner in her home somewhere in Long Island. She served ham. Grandma Rose kept a kosher home and she never ate ham even in Ukraine, in her father's house, and at home in Baltimore and New York. She was really annoyed and told me not to tell Sheldon. She did not want to hurt him. Grandma Rose kept kosher in the Golda Meir apartment and on Saturday would walk the two blocks to Temple Reyim. She enjoyed the services and remembered her early exposure to Yiddishkeit.

Once Grandma Rose invited Carolyn and Sheldon to a dinner when she lived on Neptune Avenue. As they left she offered them an apple pie to take home. Carolyn refused to accept the gift and handed it back to her because Grandma Rose used a sugar to make the pie. She used sugar sparingly to bake cakes and pies. She was really annoyed and told me not to tell Sheldon. She did not want to hurt him. At Eliot's bar mitzvah I presented Carolyn with two books for Eliot "Permission to Believe" about Judaism and the Big Bang and "Ethics of the Fathers." She threw the books back at me not wanting her son to read anything positive about Judaism.

Differing Family Philosophies

In 1972 Dorothy and I sought to buy a house. We were tired of living in an apartment with heating problems and rent increases. We purchased a 2-family house on Westbourne Terrace in Brookline. Sheldon was not happy because we collected unearned income (rent) from the tenant. Of course we paid higher taxes than single home owners, paid for electricians, plumbers, painters, and removal of two oil tanks to be replaced by use of natural gas. Sheldon was becoming a socialist with Marxist philosophy. Landlords in Russia who owned farms were called kulaks and forced to communize or be executed by the Bolsheviks.

Jonathan was born in 1975 and Carolyn asked Dorothy, when she was pregnant, if she was going to keep the fetus. Having more than two children would increase planetary pollution. Private property including farms was abolished in Russia by the Communist Government. I realized after that encounter that Carolyn could not associate with us for the following reasons: (This is my opinion). We owned a 2-family house and collected unearned income (rent). That enabled me to pay for their Jewish Education and college so they graduated without any debt. We sent our 3 children to a Hebrew Day School to learn the 4,500 years of Jewish history. After 49 years after Jonathan was born, the Wall Street Journal (5/14/2024) reports that the world birth rate has dropped below the replacement rate of 2.2 "An economy with fewer children will struggle to finance pensions and healthcare for the growing ranks of elderly." Women are encouraged to marry and have more children.

I worked for the DoD USAF and bore responsibility for bombing innocent people. I managed contracts for hardware gathering intelligence to increase national security and not develop bombs

We joined an Orthodox Synagogue and that was a waste of money and time. But what better way to learn and teach children about 4,500 years of Jewish History and attend rallies to release the Refusnicks from Russia.

Once I used Roundup to kill dandelion weeds in our front yard. Roundup contained Glyphosate which was a suspected carcinogen but proof was never accepted by the FDA (Federal Drug Administration). The dandelions never returned. I never had to use it again. Carolyn said that I was supposed to use my hands to remove dandelions.

I was not an academician and had no business offering advice on major issues. I was viewed as a non-creative lackey of corporate America since I worked for high tech corporations & Polaroid.

Sheldon's and Carolyn's Family

Carolyn had two children, Alyssa and Eliot. The first two letters of Alyssa "Al" is what everyone called Alex Krimsky. Sheldon consulted me about the name of his son. He suggested Eliot and "El" is the name of my father whose birth certificate in Russian says his name is "El" which stands for Elyosha. Eliot Krimsky is named after Alex Krimsky. Sheldon brought his children, Alyssa and Eliot to play with our kids.

Marriage of Naomi Krimsky and Yitzy Hollander

Naomi Krimsky met Yitzy Hollander and they were married in Beth El Synagogue in Newton, Massachusetts on 17 August 1993. Grandma Rose attended the wedding and asked why Carolyn Boriss Krimsky was not there. Sheldon, Alyssa, and Eliot Krimsky were all there. Carolyn was allergic to fresh paint and the walls of the wedding hall had been painted three days before the wedding. I informed her and she decided not to attend. See Figure 10.

We invited Grandma Rose to the wedding of Jonathan and Cheryl (Chaya) in New Jersey. We offered to drive her or someone would drive her so we could stay overnight for the week of blessings following a Jewish wedding. She did not feel well enough to go on such a long trip. Sheldon and Carolyn were invited but declined.

Cousin Salim's Visit to America

Cousin Salim Krimsky, son of Uncle Munya, was a noted Russian Composer of Music. Somehow he contacted Sheldon who arranged for Tufts University to play his musical compositions and pay for his airplane trip to New York. He came here twice with his two children Anna and Igor Krimsky in 1991 and 1994. I picked them up at the JFK airport and drove them twice to Boston. They stayed with us one week and with Sheldon a second week. at 60 Gorham Street in Cambridge, where he and Carolyn and their children lived. Sheldon was scheduled to pick up Salim on a Sunday morning at about 10:00 AM to go to Tufts and prepare the orchestra for the concert later that day. It was getting late and Salim was getting nervous and asked me to call Sheldon. I called and Carolyn answered the phone and berated me for calling because Sheldon is always on time. I listened and tried to explain that Salim needed confidence that Sheldon will be on time. Figure 10A. I got tired of listening to her harassment and said good bye and hung up. Sheldon heard of this and demanded an apology from me. I refused and from then on he instructed me that all phone calls to Carolyn have to go through him. That fractured our relationship. Salim, Anna and Igor spent a week in Cambridge and then a week with us.

Sheldon alone visited Salim and his children in Russia in 1991. I did not know about this until after the trip. I worked for the DoD and was told not to go to Russia. The Russians sent me photos of Sheldon's trip. Figures 11, 11A 11B, & 11C.

He met Galina, Salim's wife and Svetlana who was the wife of Igor. Anna was an accomplished pianist, and never married. Igor taught music theory and had two children, Paulina and Daniel. Paulina married a Mr. Alexander Kalinen and had one son named Boris. Daniel is married to Lola Shamirzaeva and they have no children. In 2022 Daniel ran away from a good job with a law firm in Moscow to escape to Kyrgyzstan to avoid fighting Ukrainians. He was the youngest Krimsky in Russia and now the last Krimsky in Kyrgyzstan. About one million people have left Russia at the outbreak of war with Ukraine. Some have returned but most stayed away.) Russia also has a declining birth rate. (Wall Street Journal 6/7/24) Russia ha been pursuing deserters in other countries such as Armenia by offering bonuses or punishing parents. WSJ 8/21/2024

Grandma Rose attended our Passover Seders until she almost tripped walking down the stairs to the first floor of our house. Our dining room at Westbourne Terrace was on the second floor. She feared to climb any more stairs so she spent the remaining Passovers with Sheldon and his family in Cambridge where she only had to walk up a few steps to the dining room. Alyssa, Sheldon's daughter visited Grandma Rose at the Golda Meir residence. Mom told me that she really appreciated the friendly visits. Eliot, Sheldon's son lived in New York and rarely visited her if at all. As she grew older we did take her out on Mother's day and Sheldon also took her out. We never took her out together as one family. Whenever our children and grandchildren came to see us, they always went to the Golda Meir House to visit with Grandma Rose downstairs where she provided tasty snacks for all the children. She never stopped talking about the "petzutzah." It consumed her. I kept saying to her, Mom I heard this before" and she said that: "I have to get this off my chest" but she never did."

Mom told me to stop shoveling snow when I reached 42 years old in 1978. She worried I would have a heart attack. Boston experienced 27 inches of snow. The trolleys stopped running and all schools were closed for the entire week we got warmly dressed, put Jonathan on a sled, and pulled the sled on the snow along the trolley tracks to Harvard Street to eat in a restaurant. It was a treat for all of us. The National Guard was called out by Gov. Dukakis to remove the snow from the streets. All night long we heard the noise from the front end loaders putting snow onto dump trucks for removal. I learned to not shovel snow above my head put push the snow waste high to the side. I shoveled snow from 1960 until 2013 when we moved from Brookline. The largest accumulation of snow of 92 inches was in 1987 in three different snowfalls. I shoveled the snow in our driveway so I could drive to work.

In 1999 Grandma Rose attended the retirement party for Sidney as President of the Synagogue for 12 years. She was very proud and tearful when she was mentioned as my mother. Figure 13 .

Death of Grandma Rose

In 2010 she was 95 years old. Her memory was still sharp but she suffered from vertigo and digestive problems. Her Doctor recommended Vertex as a medicine for vertigo and this worked. She went to the Newton Wellesley Hospital several times. Sheldon and his daughter Alyssa arrived at the hospital and she participated in our hospice discussions. Mom's body was failing. Once, Dr. Mark Drapkin, whom she knew, visited her to cheer her up. His wife Rosa bought her a teddy bear from the hospital gift shop. Grandma Rose said it was the first time that anyone bought her a teddy bear.

Sheldon hired Howard Block, a specialist in palliative care, to advise us about providing for Grandma Rose during what appeared to be the last few months of her life. I never met Howard Block or participated in any telephone conversations with him. I called him a few months ago in preparation for writing this book. He was retired and either did not remember or want to answer any questions. He never visited Grandma Rose at the LaSalle Nursing Home.

Sheldon and I withdrew the $32,000 that Grandma Rose saved in two trust accounts over many years as a final gift for her two boys. Sheldon and I agreed to use the funds to pay for her nursing care. The money was all used up by the La Salle nursing home for her care.

Grandma passed away just before we were to apply for Medicaid. She died penniless the same as when she arrived in the US in 1928.

I was called near midnight on Tuesday night 25 December 2012 by the nurse at La Salle to come because Grandma Rose had labored breathing, a sign of the end of life. I drove quickly to La Salle and went to her room. She lay on her back and experienced labored breathing. I did not wake her up. I asked the head nurse if she was viewed every hour because the signature boxes in the notebook were not signed. The head nurse said that this was Christmas Day and LaSalle was short of staff but she was seen every hour. The nurses were too busy to sign the visit book. The nurse said that doctor will see her on next day (Wednesday) 26 December 2012. That was the last time I saw Grandma Rose alive. The death certificate mentioned she had dementia, Figure 14. She never had dementia. She was lucid to the end. The doctor never questioned me or my brother.

The head nurse called Wednesday morning and said that Grandma Rose died Tuesday night or early Wednesday morning and I should come and pick up her belongings. Sheldon was in New York. I went and saw the empty bed. I looked at the notebook and saw that all the visits for the previous day were filled in. The head nurse also told me that the doctor never visited her but prescribed morphine to relax her labored breathing. Grandma Rose had a weak stomach and always broke her pills in half before taking them. The morphine injection dose may have been too much and may have stopped her breathing. Morphine has a risk for abuse and addiction, which can lead to overdose and death. Morphine may also cause severe, possibly fatal, breathing problems (WEB MD). I did not pursue this. I had no evidence of mistreatment so I asked no further questions of the head nurse. I removed her belongings, photos, etc. and brought everything to her apartment at the Golda Meir Housing. Figure 14.

She had been transferred to the Levine Funeral Home on Harvard Street in Brookline and underwent a tahara (washing and purification in accordance with Jewish Law). Grandma Rose paid her funeral service in advance. I was prepared to have the funeral service on Wednesday and transport Grandma Rose to her final resting place in Montefiore Cemetery in Queens but Sheldon and Carolyn were in New York. The wanted some friends to attend the service who also lived in New York. We decided to have the service at Levine's Chapel on Friday early morning and then transport Grandma Rose via hearse to the Montefiore Cemetery on Sunday morning. Eulogies at the chapel were given by me, Rabbi Elly Krimsky, Rabbi Jonathan Krimsky, and Dorothy. Naomi spoke at the gravesite. Their eulogies are recorded in the book "From Brooklyn, NY to Brookline, MA." Sheldon and Carolyn did not speak. Dorothy sat in the hearse as the guardian and we drove quickly to the cemetery. She was buried near Alex, her husband for 31 years. Eliot Krimsky threw a red rose on the coffin as it was lowered into the grave. I wanted to return to Brookline before sundown. Sheldon and his family stayed in New York. I drove quickly to Brookline and arrived just before Sundown to begin the seven days of shiva.. Carolyn had an apartment in Greenwich Village so Sheldon drove to Manhattan. I sat shiva for a week at home. Shul members brought a Torah carried in the arc that I built about two years earlier for such purposes. I was the first to use the arc I built.

Red roses symbolize deep respect, courage, and strength, making them a meaningful choice to express love and admiration for the deceased. They are commonly used in funeral arrangements for close family members or friends and can be incorporated into casket sprays, standing sprays, and funeral bouquets. In the movie "The GodFather", the heads of mafia families all placed a red rose on the casket of Vito Corleone (played by Marlon Brando), the GodFather.

The management at Golda Meir House told us we had about two weeks to empty Grandma Rose's apartment. Dorothy, Sheldon, Annette

Pechenik (friend of Dorothy's) and I empted her apartment. We gave her clothes to a charity. We took a large mirror and a smaller hall mirror and photographs and Jewish prayer books. She did attend synagogue services on Saturday mornings at Temple Reyim, a few minute walk from the Golda Meir House. I donated the books to the Brighton Beach Synagogue on Ocean Parkway. There were no discussions or disagreements between Sheldon and us about what to take from her apartment. Grandma Rose's gravesite is shown in Figure 15.

I offered many times to drive Sheldon to the gravesite from Jamaica Station when he did not drive his car to New York. He ignored my offer. I don't believe he ever visited his mother's or his father's gravesite after their funerals. Visits to gravesites are a sign of respect. Visitors usually leave small stones at the site showing that they were there. Her legacy from my side (Krimsky-Skolnick) shows great-grandchildren and great-great grandchildren of whom five males will carry the Krimsky name into the 22st Century. I am not familiar with relatives from the Boriss side. Figure 16. From Sheldon's side there are no male Krimskys. Figure 17.

Death of Sheldon Krimsky

This section is primarily prepared for Siona Rose Krimsky to learn seomething about hr grandfather, Sheldon. He was a person of great honesty and integrity. He died suddenly on Sunday 10 April 2012 in Cambridge from a bowel obstruction. According to doctors with whom I spoke, that condition means that the intestines are entangled and food does not flow freely. This is a rare condition but it does happen and is painful. The phone call from Eliot to Alec came about a week after he was buried in Woodlawn Cemetery in the Bronx. There was supposed to be a memorial service at Tufts University. I tried to attend and I called the director of the research facility. I was told that the service was only for immediate family members. Sheldon died alone at Mt Auburn Hospital in Cambridge. I was informed by Alec and Naomi that he died and was already buried but not told where. I was not informed or invited to a funeral or memorial service. Figure 18 shows his death certificate. We located his grave and visited the cemetery in June 2023 and there was no memorial stone. The cemetery administrator told me at that time that they had no request for a memorial stone and any such memorial had to be approved by his wife. I sent photographs of the gravesite without a memorial stone to Alyssa and Eliot but received no response. Figure 19. In April 2024 the gravesite shows a name plate in preparation for placing a memorial stone. Figures 20 & 21. Figure 17 is a brief biography of Sheldon as I knew him as a secular humanist, honest, incorruptible, technically rigorous, prolific, and sensitive to financial, social and political issues that corrupt science. Secular humanism is defined by Noah Feldman in his book "To Be A Jew Today." The New York Times devoted ¼ page to his obituary. Sheldon had 2 children, 3 grandchildren, 5 cousins, 7 aunts, 7 uncles, some of whom we never met, two parents and one brother from the Krimsky-Skolnick sides.

Rabbi Moshe Taragin in his book "Dark Clouds Above, Faith Below" defines the three generations of Jews emerging from challenging circumstances (Bolshevik Revolution and Anti Semitism in Russia). The first generation is motivated to accumulate sustenance, knowledge, & wealth. They survived by emigrating to America. Zadie Skolnick is an example of that generation. The second generation consolidates the sustenance, knowledge and produces more wealth. His three children are examples. Grandma Rose was the second generation although she married a house painter and never accumulated much wealth. She did consolidate her knowledge by maintaining a kosher home, sending her two children to Talmud Torah, paid for our education and paid attention when I lit the Chanukah Candles that she enjoyed watching. Aunt Rae purchased the chrome plated Chanukah Menorah. Later Grandma attended High Holiday and Sabbath services at the Synagogue on Ocean Parkway when she lived alone on Neptune Avenue. Zadie's children had no interest in Judaism. The third generation takes everything for granted and either squanders the wealth or accumulates knowledge and professional achievement to achieve the American Dream. This is an accurate picture of what happened to me. The third generation from Zadie Skolnick ignored the Jewish influence from their grandfather. My cousins Mark, Linda, Steven, Michael and Richard had no connection with Judaism. The Krimskys from Russia were deprived of any Jewish education and it had little or no influence on the children of the third generation. They will disappear from the pages of Jewish history. Only my children, grand children and great grandchildren will carry the knowledge of 4,500 years of Jewish learning into the 22nd century and beyond. Grandma Rose never lost her Jewish roots and her legacy will continue into the 22nd century. Her three Krimsky grandchildren married, bought beautiful single family homes, sent their children to Hebrew Day Schools, travel and revel in the American Dream. Grandma Rose would be proud.

References:

"From Brooklyn, NY to Brookline, MA" by Sidney Krimsky Copyright 2022

"My Life as a Motherless Child" by Sheldon Krimsky Copyright 2002

"Dark Clouds Above, Faith Below" by Rabbi Moshe Taragin Copyright 2024

Other books published by Sheldon Krimsky and Sidney Krimsky are listed on the last page.

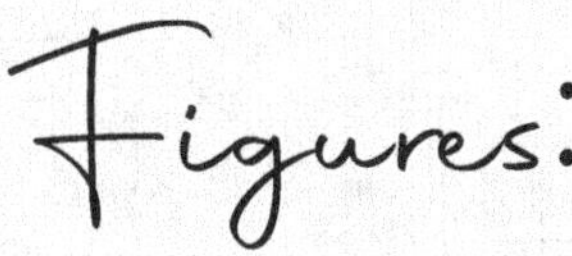 Figures:

Figure 1. Torah Mantle . Purchasing a Torah and cover (mantel) is an accepted and appreciated long time Jewish custom to honor and show respect for a deceased person. The persons honored are Grandma Jennie Reisman, grandmother of Yitzy Hollander and Grandma Rose Krimsky, grandmother of Naomi (Krimsky) Hollander.

Figure 2. Front of 456 Alabama Avenue in East New York, home of Isadore Skolnick, her father, and Rose before her marriage.

Figure 3. Inside of 456 Alabama Avenue. The Skolnicks lived on the right side at the end of the corridor. The hallway has been modernized.

Figure 4. New apartment building opposite 456. It sits exactly on the site of the Shul where Rose and Alex were married.

Figure 5. Front of 496 Williams Avenue where Alex and Rose lived after they were married. Outside has been modernized

Figure 6. Photo of Krimskys and Skolnicks at the Melrose Chateau, site of Sidney's bar mitzvah party: Standing left to right: Rose, Alex, Sheldon, Grandpa Isadore Skolnick, Sidney and Bubbe Anna Skolnick, the "putzutzah." During my

infrequent trips to Alabama Avenue, my grandfather (Zaidy) told me that he goes to Shul every Shabbos and bought "psicha" which is the privilege of opening the arc for removal of the Torah scroll for reading. The "psicha" and other honors are auctioned off to the highest bidder to help pay for the annual Shul operating expenses.

Figure 7. Ad for Camel Cigarettes that appeared on TV and subway cars. I believed it was a lie but people smoked Camels. These ads appeared on the New York subways above the seats and later on TV sets. The ads claim that more doctors smoke Camels than any other cigarette. My father smoked Camels outside our apartment. So we never breathed second hand smoke. Cigarettes were expensive and I always viewed putting any foreign substance into your throat was stupid. So I never smoked. I walked on the Boardwalk in Coney Island almost every day and breathed fresh air.

Figure 8. Photo of Grandma Rose, Alex, Sidney and Sheldon standing on the John W. Weeks Bridge crossing over the Charles River in Cambridge Massachusetts a few blocks from my apt at 1200 Mass Avenue that connects Cambridge to Allston, a suburb of Boston in May 1965 to attend my graduation from Northeastern University with an MSME degree.

Figure 9. Photo of Grandma Rose at her departure party from Neptune Avenue held at Ratner's Restaurant on the Lower East Side of New York

Figure 10. Photo of our relatives at the wedding of Naomi and Yitzy Hollander in Beth El in Newton, Massachusetts. Standing left to right: Sheldon, Jonathan, Sidney, Yitzy, Naomi, Dorothy, Alec, & Eliot. Seated are Alyssa & Grandma Rose. Carolyn (Boriss) Krimsky could not attend because the wedding hall was freshly painted three days before the wedding and she was allergic to fresh paint. She decided not to attend.

Figure 10A. Seated in Sheldon's home in Cambridge 1991 during Salim's visit: left to right: Carolyn, Eliot, Sheldon,

Salim & Igor Krimsky.

Figure 11. Relatives in Russia. Left to right: Igor: Sheldon, Daniel, Svetlana, Anna, & Salim Krimsky outside Salim's or Igor's apartment in Moscow.

Figure 11A Igor, Daniel, & Salim Krimsky standing in front of St Basil's Cathedral in Red Square (Красная площадь)

Figure 11B Sheldon and Munya Krimsky in Moscow

Figure 11C Relatives in Russia: Seated left to right: Salim, Munya, Daniel, Svetlana, Sheldon, Anna

Figure 12. Celebration of Sid's retirement as Shul President for 12 years. He was honored at a special Retirement party in November 1999. Grandma Rose was present and felt proud of her oldest son. Standing from left to right Rabbi Abraham Halbfinger, Spiritual advisor and full-time rabbi of the synagogue, Alec (Elly) Krimsky, Sidney Krimsky, Jonathan Krimsky, Yitzy Hollander. Seated below: Rebbitzen Silvia Halbfinger, Dorothy Krimsky, Naomi Krimsky holding Simma Hollander, and Grandma Rose Krimsky. Seated children left to right are Ephraim Hollander and Joseph (Yossi) Hollander. Rabbi Elly Krimsky made a beautiful speech about me.

Figure 13. Russian relatives on a boat trip on the Moscow River. Right to left: Svetlana Krimsky (wife of Igor), Igor Krimsky, Galina (I think) wife of Salim), Unknown person, Daniel and his wife Lola Krimsky, Mr. Kalinen and his wife Paulina (I think). Paulina is the daughter of Igor and Svetlana & Daniel is the son of Igor and Svetlana. Salim is probably the photographer.

Figure 14. Death certificate of Grandma Rose. She may have had pneumonia. She had labored breathing the last time I saw her. I never believed she had dementia. The staff nurse lied to me when she said that Grandma Rose was seen every hour on 25 December 2012.by an attendant. The staff was shorthanded on Christmas day. The staff nurse said the doctor would visit her in the morning on 26 December. He did not visit her. He prescribed morphine to ease her breathing. The morphine overloaded her frail body and she stopped breathing. The certificate says that Sheldon was the informant. He was the health care proxy but never consulted me except to ask me to surrender $16,000 for Mom's hospice care. Mom left $32,000 to both of us and Sheldon used his money first to pay LaSalle Nursing Home and Howard Block for hospice care. I surrendered the funds for her hospice care.

Figure 15. Gravestone of Grandma Rose Krimsky in the Montifiore Cemetery near Alex Krimsky

Figure 16. Legacy of Grandma Rose. Wedding of Simma Hollander and Avi Martin. Attending were 16 Krimskys & 5 young male Krimskys. This family photo shows the Krimsky and Hollander families at the wedding of Avi Martin and Simma Hollander. Attending the wedding but not in the photo are Yedidiah and Yocheved Krimsky. I view all our family as truly amazing. Dorothy and Sidney were married on 14 August 1966 at the Regency House in Queens. We started life with one apartment, one car, three college degrees, and one job. Over the years three children expanded to 14 grandchildren and today four great-grandchildren. This is truly amazing to see this unfolding before our very eyes.

Figure 17. Genealogy chart of Sidney and Sheldon Krimsky.

Grandma Rose met them all except Yakira, Shoshana, & Reuvain. I don't know if she met Lisa Bengar & Siona. The three grandchildren were born after her passing. Grandma Rose met all her grand-children and most of her great-grandchildren. Four great-grandchildren were born after she passed away. They are Shoshana Reizel Krimsky, Reuvain Krimsky, Yakira Krimsky and Siona Rose Krimsky. The three girls are named after Grandma Rose. Reuvain was named after his great-grandfather, Reuvain Lazarus. On my side, the five Krimsky boys will carry the Jewish tradition into the 22nd century. They are Aryeh Leib, Yedidiah, Shai, Akiva, and Reuvain Krimsky.

The Russians in the Ukraine were probably required to take second names around 1600 by the Tzar when they lived in the Crimea. In Russian, Crimea is spelled Krym pronounced Krum in Russian and Krim in Ukrainian. Sky in Russian means "from" or "associated with." So the name Krimsky means from the Crimea.

Samuel Krimsky married Sonya Feldman, They had 5 children, two boys Munya and Elyosha (Alex). Munya married Frieda and had one son, Salim Krimsky named after Samuel Krimsky who died in 1930. Salim married Galina and they had two children, Igor and Anna. Anna was a concert pianist and never married. Igor married Svetlana and had two children, Paulina and Daniel. Paulina married Alexander Kalinen and had one son named Boris Kalinen. Daniel married Lola and had no children. Daniel Krimsky worked in a law firm in Moscow. He knew computers and communicated with me in English on the internet. About 3 years ago he emailed me that he was leaving for Kygerstan. I presume that he did not want to be in the Russian army and kill Ukrainians. The Krimsky name will disappear in Russia in the 22nd century. If Daniel returns to Russia he will be arrested for desertion. He stopped sending me emails because they can be traced back to him. Only from my side will the Krimsky name be perpetuated into the 22nd century.

Figure 18. Death certificate of Sheldon Krimsky, (two pages). His death came as a shock to me. An autopsy was performed. His family would not tell me where he was buried. I was not informed of any funeral service. I learned from other sources that he was buried in the Woodlawn Cemetery in the Bronx, NY. About 10 days after he died. He was 5 years younger than me and never complained to me about any physical problems. He was active as a University Professor. He wrote about 14 books at Tufts University. The last two were about DNA and Ancestry and Conflicts of Interest in Science because of funding and political pressure. Both books were based on considerable research. The DNA Book is highly technical and suitable for experts in the field of DNA research.

Figure 19. Gravesite of Sheldon Krimsky in Woodlawn Cemetery, 517 East 233rd Street, Bronx, NY 10470 -2401.

Alpine Hill, Section 174, Lot 381, Grave # 1, West Side of Heather Avenue June 2022

Figure 20. Burial Site April 2024 with a grave marker.

Figure 21. Burial site April 2024 showing a grave marker

This is my last email to Sheldon in 2020 before he passed away.

Sheldon,

Enclosed is a copy of my third book "Leaving Mother Russia" now available on Amazon. I included immigration struggles of our parents, grandfather, and Fishel Fiedel who is a cousin of our father.

Our family has all been vaccinated except for children under 11 years old. I have received the Pfizer booster. Jonathan and Alec had mild cases of Coved before vaccinations. Dorothy and I had no reactions to vaccinations and we were tested twice for Coved and the results were negative. We are no longer required to wear masks while shopping or eating in restaurants in Nassau County. New York City has stricter rules.

I visited Coney Island recently and could not believe all the changes. Mermaid Avenue with storefront stores has been restored and Surf Avenue is filled with high rise apartment buildings. Large apartment buildings have been near the boardwalk and there is no access to the beach under the boardwalk because the area has been filled with sand. I walked all over Kaiser Park and the handball courts and tennis courts are as they were 75 years ago but the ball fields have changed. Kaiser Park has been extended North and there is a beach on the South side of Coney Island Creek accessible from Kaiser Park that leads to Sea Gate. Soil has been dumped and trees planted where there used to be water. Neptune Avenue between Stillwell Avenue and Mark Twain JHS is being torn up and repaired. The building that housed the Brooklyn Gas Company is no longer in use.

Sid Krimsky
Brief Biography of Sheldon by his brother Figure 25

June 26, 2022

Sheldon Krimsky was born to Alex and Rose Krimsky in June 1941. He was named after his grandfather, Shalom Krimsky, later anglicized to Samuel who migrated to the US in 1911. Samuel died in 1930. Samuel sent money for Alex and his sister to emigrate in 1924 and the sisters and mother in 1926. Alex, 3 sisters and one brother lived in the village of Tulchin in Southern Ukraine. Their mother worked as a cook in an orphanage. Alex was shot in the leg by armed Cossacks during a pogrom. Alex had about 2-3 years of schooling. The emigrations of Alex and Rose are described in the book "From Brooklyn, NY to Brookline, MA" and "Leaving Mother Russia."

Rose was born and lived in Bieleh, a small village near the town of Yampol north of the Crimea in Ukraine. Her mother died when Rose was about 4 years old. She was raised by two aunts. She had no shoes and attended no school. Her father emigrated to the USA on the day she was born to avoid conscription. Her father sent money for her to immigrate to the USA when Rose was about 13 years old. Bieleh was probably eviscerated by the Nazis who invaded Ukraine. She learned to read and write and arithmetic during the few years she attended school. Rose was withdrawn from Junior High School and not allowed to graduate because the family needed income. Alex Krimsky worked as a metal worker in the Baltimore Naval Shipyard during WW II, house painter and later as a taxi driver in New York until he developed a heart condition. We had money for food, and rent, and basic clothing. Education in the New York City public schools and colleges were free. Sheldon and I grew up in Coney

Island in three small rooms with an inside bathroom. He attended PS 188 and Mark Twain JHS. He played street games and followed the Brooklyn Dodgers. We took the subway to Ebbets Field and watched the Dodgers play the Pittsburgh Pirates at a double header and saw Ralph Kiner hit a home run. Sheldon even walked with me to visit our grandfather in East New York on the Jewish Day of Atonement. He was studious and was selected to attend Stuyvesant HS.

Sheldon was a sensitive soul. That is why our mother selected him to be her health care proxy. She died at age 98.5 and Sheldon interrupted his academic work to be in charge of her care. At age 9 or 10 he asked our parents to buy a canary and bird cage and he would provide food, water and clean the cage. Cary the Canary died 6 or 8 months later and he felt sad and our sensitive mother did not want to just throw the dead bird into the trash. So I made a cardboard box for Cary, brought Cary to an adjacent empty lot with weeds and trees, dug a hole, placed the box into the hole, and covered the hole with dirt to prevent rodents from eating the bird. I recited the Hebrew prayer for the dead over the bird and Sheldon felt better. Sheldon asked for another bird so our parents bought a parakeet that we named Fogel. The same thing happened in 6 or 8 months. We buried Fogel and gave away the bird cage.

He attended Brooklyn College majoring in physics following in my footsteps. Our immigrant parents were poor and Sheldon realized that education was the only way to achieve the American Dream. He was not influenced by money or power but was a pursuer of truth and this was reflected in his PhD thesis about the philosophy of science using thought experiments in which he examined space, time, and vacuum idealizations and their consequence for tangible experiments and idealized physical laws. He wrote 17 books about environmental hazards, GMOs, DNA, pesticides in food, etc. subjects that were not taught in school and not reflected in his PhD thesis. He must have attended lectures, consulted with colleagues, read and understood learned articles before he gained a prodigious understanding of these subjects. He exposed the influence of money on science even in academia. He was responsible for having authors reveal their sources of funding in technical papers and conferences to reveal any potential influences from the funding source. He was a pioneer in exposing the influence of money on scientific results. Sheldon was rational, honest, and incorruptible, a product of poor uneducated parents and the free New York City public school system. A lounge library at Tufts has been named in his honor. Figure 31. A more extensive biography may be found on-line by entering his name in the tool bar as SheldonKrimskyMemorial. He is also the grandfather of Siona Rose Krimsky.

SidneyKrimsky
June 2022

Figure 26

Addresses:

Addresses whose sum of digits equals 15 are lucky places because the sum of the words used in the priestly blessing equals 15. 3, 5, & 7 are the number of words in the three priestly blessings and the sum equals 15. Here is a list of old addresses with which Krimsky's were associated.

Can you guess what they represent or who lived there?

217   Watkins Avenue

496   Williams Avenue

637   Blake Avenue

456   Alabama Avenue

2995   West 29th Street

1321   K Street

357   Walton Street

517   East 23rd Street

255   Herring Court

169   Dumont Avenue

517   East 233rd Street

60   Gorham Street

19   Eden Road

202   Patricia Place

310   Plymouth Street

1200   Mass Avenue

108   Westbourne Terrace

321   Summit Avenue

403   Washington Street

11   Oak Knis Street

11527 Morning Grove Drive

49   Roseland Street

111   Irving Place

400   East 17th Street

42   Loveland Road

25   Nevo Street

2   Endo Boulevard

1   Chiswick Terrace

75   Wallingford Road

147 - 21 71st Avenue

147 - 40 70th Road

147 - 35 76th Street

101   Washington Street

195   Corey Road

103   Westbourne Terrace

750   Washington Street

34   Philbrick Road

125   Wells Avenue

88   Nottinghill Road

129   Clark Road

310   Summit Avenue

184   Lancaster Terrace

271   Summit Avenue

193   Chiswick Road

11   Williston Road

410   Harvard Street

1710   Beacon Street

62   Green Street

324   Harvard Street

428   Harvard Street

15   Washington Street

324   Harvard Street

428   Harvard Street

15   Washington Street

Figure 27

Books published by Sidney Krimsky:

From Brooklyn, NY to Brookline, MA

Untaught Math

Leaving Mother Russia

Blood Testing and Analysis

Biography of Grandma Rose

Books published by Sheldon Krimsky

Environmental Hazards –Communicating Risks as a Social Process

Conflicts of Interest in Science –How Corporate Funded Academic Research Can Threaten Public Health

Understanding DNA Ancestry

Genetic Alchemy – The Social History of the Recombinant DNA Controversy

GMOs Decoded

Genetic Justice-DNA Data Banks

Hormonal Chaos

Science in the Private Interest

Biotechnics and Society – Rise of Industrial Genetics

Rights and Liberties in the Bio Tech Ages

Stem Cell Dialogues – A Philosophical & Scientific Inquiry into Medical Frontiers

Environmental Hazards

Agricultural Biotechnology for the Environment

Social Theories of Risk

Figure 28 shows the corrugated washboard used to wash clothing in a bathtub and the hand-operated meat grinder used to make hamburgers and meatballs that I enjoyed disassembling and cleaning after each time it was used.

Figure 29 shows the wooden bowl Mom used to chop fish and the hand chopper. Also shown is the stool she used to access the special Passover dishes located on the top shelves of the kitchen cabinets. Sometimes I would stand on the stool and hand her the dishes.

Figure 30 is a photograph of 2995 West 29th Street before demolition.

Figure 31 is a photograph of the sign outside the Tufts University lounge dedicated to Sheldon Krimsky.

Figure 32 is a photograph of the gravestone of Sheldon Krimsky installed about 2 1/2 years after his death. There are no Jewish symbols on the gravestone. It is customary in Jewish tradition to have a graveside memorial service, attended by colleagues, relatives, and friends by unveiling a curtain around the gravestone. I was not invited and doubt if such a ceremony was held.

ועתה
כתבו לכם
את
השירה
הזאת
לעילוי נשמות
שיינא דבורה בת
הרב יצחק יעקב ע״ה
רייזל בת יצחק ע״ה

Figure 1

Figure 2

Figure 3

Figure 4

Figure 5

Figure 6

Figure 6A

According to a recent Nationwide survey:
MORE DOCTORS SMOKE CAMELS THAN ANY OTHER CIGARETTE
CAMEL
Your "T-Zone" Will Tell You...
T for Taste...
T for Throat...
CAMELS Costlier Tobaccos

18

Figure 7

Figure 8

Figure 9

Figure 10

Figure 10A

Figure 11

Figure 11A

Figure 11B

Figure 11C

Figure 12

Figure 13

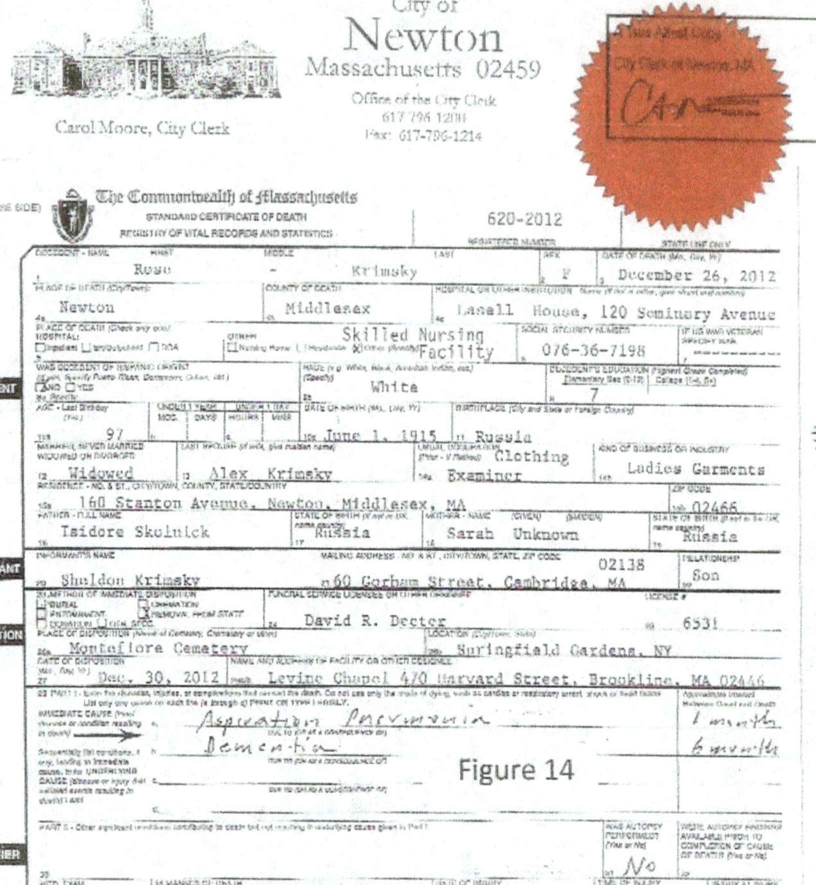
Figure 14

Figure 15

Rose
Krimsky
Beloved Wife
Dear Mother
Beloved Grandmother
Great-Grandmother
June 1914
Dec 26, 2012

edding of Simma Hollander and Avi Martin on 28   March 2022

Krimsky Hollander Family
Seating left to right
Rabbi Jonathan Krimsky
Cheryl (Chaya) Krimsky
Reuvain Krimsky held by Cheryl
Sidney Krimsky
Shoshana Krimsky held by Sid Krimsky
Dorothy Krimsky
Yossi Hollander
Yoshua Hollander held by Yossi
Meira Hollander
Yakira Krimsky
Standing left to right
Tziporah Krimsky
Akiva Krimsky
Aryeh Leib Krimsky(next to Tziporah)
Ephraim Hollander
Leah Hollander
Naomi Hollander
Simma Martin (wedding photo)
Avraham (Avi) Martin (wedding photo)
Yitzy Hollander
Tamar Hollander
Yaakov Yedidiah Krimsky
Yocheved Krimsky
Rachlie Krimsky
Rabbi Alec (Elly) Krimsky
Yeshaya (Shai) Krimsky
Malka Krimsky

Figure 16

Alex & Rose (Skolnick) Krimsky
Sidney
Sheldon
Sidney & Dorothy (Goldstein) Krimsky
Sheldon & Carolyn (Boriss) Krimsky
Alec
Naomi
Jonathan
Alyssa (Krimsky) & William Clossey
Andrew
Benjamin
Eliot & Lisa (Bengar) Krimsky
Alec & Yocheved (Zionis) Krimsky
Siona
Yedidiah
Rachelie
Yakira
Naomi (Krimsky) & Yitzy Hollander
Ephraim
Joseph
Simma
Tamar
Jonathan & Cheryl (Lazarus) Krimsky
Aryeh
Tziporah
Shai
Malka
Akiva
Shoshana
Reuvain
Ephraim & Leah (Fruchter) Hollander
Joseph & Meira (David) Hollander
Avi & Simma (Hollander) Martin
Naftali
Shua
Shaina
Asher

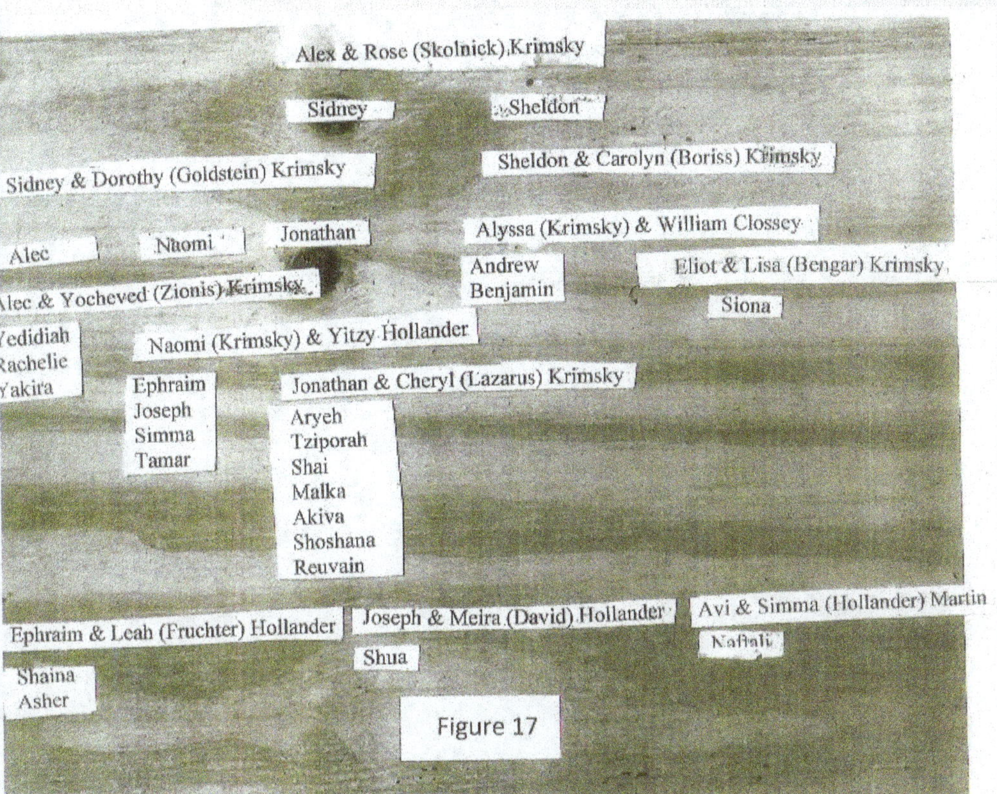

Figure 17

CERTIFICATE OF VITAL RECORD

VERIFY PRESENCE OF WATERMARK   HOLD TO LIGHT TO VIEW

The Commonwealth of Massachusetts

CT 5981946

Commonwealth of Massachusetts
Registry of Vital Records and Statistics
CERTIFICATE OF DEATH

State File # 2022 021187
Registered # 305

Place of Death	MT. AUBURN HOSPITAL, CAMBRIDGE, MA
Date of Death	APRIL 23, 2022 — Age 80 YRS — Sex MALE
Current Name	KRIMSKY, SHELDON —
Surname at Birth or Adoption	KRIMSKY — SSN 116-30-0198
AKA	—
Date of Birth	JUNE 26, 1941 — Birthplace BROOKLYN, NEW YORK
Residence	60 GORHAM STREET, CAMBRIDGE, MASSACHUSETTS 02138
Race	WHITE
Education	DOCTORATE OR PROFESSIONAL DEGREE
Marital Status	MARRIED
Occupation/Industry	PROFESSOR/EDUCATION

Last Spouse – Last, First, Middle (Surname at Birth or Adoption)
BORISS-KRIMSKY, CAROLYN (PROBSTEIN)

Decedent: U.S. Veteran (Most Recent)
NO

Parent Name – Last, First, Middle (Surname at Birth or Adoption)
KRIMSKY, ROSE (SHKOLNICK) — Birthplace **RUSSIA**

Parent Name – Last, First, Middle (Surname at Birth or Adoption)
KRIMSKY, ALEX (KRIMSKY) — Birthplace **RUSSIA**

Part I. Cause of Death – Sequentially list immediate cause then antecedent causes then underlying cause — Interval between onset and death

a. Immediate Cause (Final condition resulting in death)
PULSELESS ELECTRICAL ACTIVITY ARREST — — HRS.

b. Due to or as a consequence of:
SMALL BOWEL OBSTRUCTION WITH POSSIBLE ASPIRATION — — HRS.

c. Due to or as a consequence of: —

d. Due to or as a consequence of:

Part II. Other significant conditions contributing to death but not resulting in underlying cause
—

Manner of Death: **NATURAL**
Time of Death: **06:27 PM**
Result of Injury: **NO**

Certifier **GUILLAUME CHEBION, MD** — Lic # 285311
Addr. **330 MOUNT AUBURN STREET, CAMBRIDGE, MASSACHUSETTS 02138**

Funeral Licensee/Designee **JULIE BERGER** — Lic # 50744
Facility/Addr. **LEVINE CHAPEL, BROOKLINE, MASSACHUSETTS**
Immediate Disposition **BURIAL**
Date of Immediate Disposition **APRIL 29, 2022**
Place/Address
WOODLAWN CEMETERY, 4199 WEBSTER AVENUE, BRONX, NEW YORK 10470
Date of Record **MAY 02, 2022**
Date of Amendment —

Anthony d Wilson
CLERK, CITY OF CAMBRIDGE

DATE ISSUED: OCTOBER 02, 2023

I, the undersigned, hereby certify that I am the Clerk of the City of Cambridge; that as such I have custody of the records of birth, marriage, and death required by law to be kept in my office; and I do hereby certify that the above is a true copy from said records, as held in the Commonwealth's central vital records information repository.

Figure 18

Clerk
City of Cambridge

R-301 p. 2 of 2   KRIMSKY   SFN: 2022 021187

CAMBRIDGE 305

CAMBRIDGE

STATE VOL/PG: 39/183 OPEN

If U.S. war veteran, specify war/conflict(s) —		
Branch of military (most recent) —	Rank/organization/outfit(most recent) —	
Date entered(most recent) —	Date Discharged (most recent) —	Service Number(most recent) —
Place of Death Type **HOSPITAL - INPATIENT**	Date of Pronouncement —	Time of Pronouncement —
RN/NP/PA Pronouncement? **NO**	Name of RN/NP/PA Pronouncing Death —	Lic # —
RN/NP/PA Employing Agency or Institution —	Name of Physician or Medical Examiner notified —	
Was M.E. Notified? **NO**	Provider in charge of patient's care, if not certifier **ALEXANDRA FILIPPI, MD**	
Autopsy Performed? **YES**	Findings available for Cause? **NO**	Tobacco contribute to death? **UNKNOWN**	Pregnancy Status, if female —
Date of Injury —	Time of Injury —	Injury at Work? —	If Transportation Injury, specify: —
Place of Injury —	Location/Address of Injury: —	
Describe How Injury Occurred		
Expanded Race: **WHITE**		
Ethnicity: **AMERICAN**		
Informant Name **ELIOT — KRIMSKY** Addr. **400 E 17TH STREET, #700, BROOKLYN, NEW YORK 11226**		Relationship **SON**
Date Disposition Permit Issued: **APRIL 28, 2022**	Board of Health Agent **DERRICK L. NEAL**	
State Tracking No. **021187**	Local Permit No. **22-021187**	

Figure 18 A

Figure 19

Figure 20

Figure 22

This is Bessie, a friend of Rose Skolnick

circa 1934 – 1935. We never met her.

Figure 24

Some of the Krimsky Second Cousins of Siona Rose whom she never met. Photo circa 2016.

Figure 25

Figure 28

Figure 29

figure 30

2995 West 29th Street in Coney Island. Entrance way to the courtyard with four staircases at each corner. We lived on the right side furthest corner 2nd floor in three rooms. We sat on the white capstones and played territory (with a knife) in the yard between the capstones and the building. Mr Koten, building owner and his family, lived on the left side first floor.

His windows were open during the summer months. Mr. Wenig's grocery store is on the lower right of the photograph. Pickles cost a nickel.

Figure 31

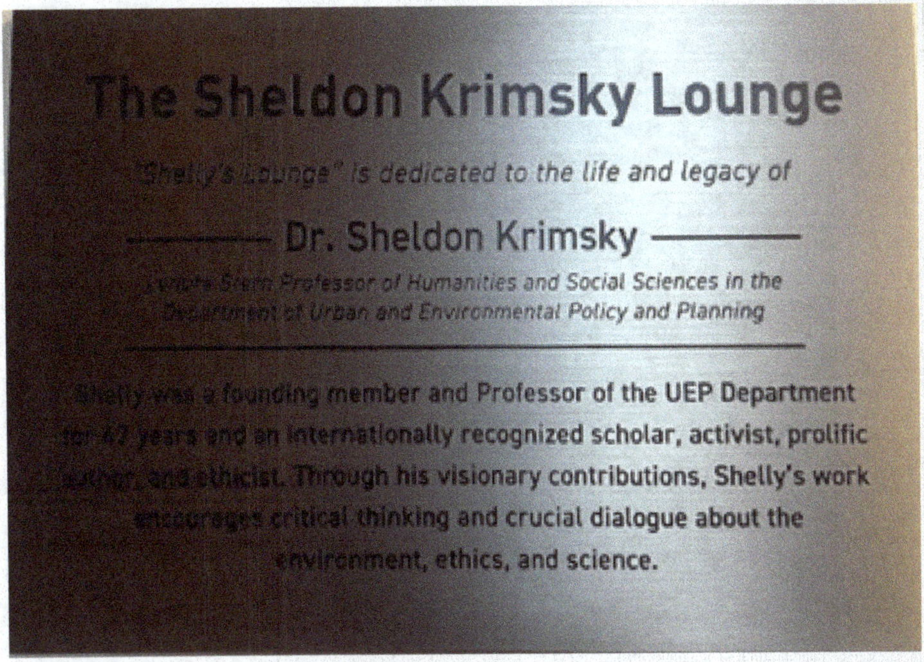

The lounge is symbolic of the intellectual legacy we inherited from Professor Sheldon Krimsky

Figure 32

August 2024 An unmarked grave is the final destiny of Prof Sheldon Krimsky. The orange flags indicate that someone is buried below the ground